THE LOCUST YEARS

THE LOCUST YEARS

poems

Paul J. Pastor

Wiseblood Books

Copyright © 2025 Paul J. Pastor

All rights reserved, including the right to reproduce this book or any portions thereof in any form whatsoever except for brief quotations in book reviews. For information, address the publisher:

>   Wiseblood Books
>   Post Office Box 870
>   Menomonee Falls, Wisconsin 53052

Cover and interior art by Michael Cook, used with permission
Cover lettering by Jacob Cowdin/SPACE DEPARTMENT
Typesetting by Rhonda Ortiz

ISBN: 978-1-951319-04-5 (hardcover)
       978-1-951319-03-8 (paperback)

Also by Paul J. Pastor:

Spiritual and Devotional

The Face of the Deep
The Listening Day, Volume One
The Listening Day, Volume Two

Poetry

Bower Lodge: Poems

For Emily, forever.

Rise up; the realm of love renews
the battle it was born to lose.

—Geoffrey Hill

Contents

Letter from Paul

The Springs

- 5 · Skookumchuck
- 6 · Regarding Spring, Which Sharpens Grief by Means of Fresh, Unconquerable Joys
- 7 · Nehalem
- 8 · The Child's Teeth
- 9 · What May Not Be Accepted
- 10 · The Mole
- 11 · Here is a tiny dance; you cannot force it.
- 12 · Of Bracken, and Other Natural Fractals, as an Image of the Unfurling Soul
- 13 · Up the Sun, Down the Moon
- 14 · The Early Road
- 15 · Two Stanzas (for Emily)
- 16 · Photosynthesis
- 17 · The Hope of Tears
- 18 · The Noise of the Groat
- 19 · Who Has Been a Friend?

The Summers

- 25 · Montana Seeds
- 26 · Damascus Road
- 27 · Annus Mirabilis
- 29 · Where the Kildeer Runs
- 30 · Below the Glen
- 31 · American Isolate

32 · Wringing the Changes
33 · Wild Currants, *or* How Sorrow is the School of Wisdom
34 · On Wasted Time
35 · Zoetrope of Paul
36 · Chariot of Elijah
37 · Notes For a Poem (To a Dead Friend)
38 · On Wauna Lake
39 · Of a Hermit Thrush
40 · The Night Garden
41 · Under the Perseids
42 · The Dream
43 · Crosses

The Falls

49 · Phantom Limb
50 · The Alembic
51 · The Locust Years
53 · For V. the Bag Lady, Great in the Kingdom of Heaven
54 · Because I Thought That Hope Was Not for Me
55 · The Visitation
56 · Blue Bandana
57 · The Garden of Abu Ghosh
58 · I Must Become as Beautiful as Kelp
59 · By This You'll Know It's Love
60 · Sawgrass Song
61 · A Small Defiance
62 · In the Fall
63 · The Oracle
64 · On Crucifixion as Holding One Open from the Instinctive Fetal Position of the Wounded
65 · That Which Cannot Rest Content
66 · Lachrymae Mundi
67 · Cherry On, Lost John

68 · Haunting
69 · Hunting
70 · Grinding the Peppercorns
71 · Growing Late

The Winters

77 · The Winter Bank
78 · The Watch
79 · Staying
80 · Every Upping is a Down
81 · A Song for Late in Time
82 · Science of Relations
85 · Advice
86 · Gap of the Hedge
87 · Snowed In
88 · Surely, a Well Feels like a Wound to the Earth
89 · The Cameo
90 · Let Us Keep the Feast
91 · St. Erzsébet Daydreams of a Lost Swallow
92 · I Have Visited the Country on the Other Side of Grief
93 · Too Quick the Thaw
94 · Exchange Rate
95 · Severing Road
97 · Some lines written after realizing that time may be simply a vast loom, and our lives its colored threads.
98 · To One Who Would Mourn Me
99 · Talus
100 · The Sower

Acknowledgments
About the Author
About the Artist

Dear Reader,

The poems in this book were written mostly between 2020 and the middle of 2024. Those years were difficult for many people, but they were, for reasons that are quietly private, the most difficult of my life. People trying to decode some specific biography here will be disappointed—though much of the work orbits particular "unfixable" griefs, in these pages are poems about all *sorts* of other things, pleasant and unpleasant. This is because large difficulties have a sort of magnetic and seasonal effect in our lives. They do things. They *move* things. They come and go on somewhat predictable schedules. They make their own weather. You cannot set a clock by them, but sometimes you can set a calendar, or a compass.

In the early versions I drafted of this little book, I had, at various times, at least three different opening quotations before settling on the one you just read from Geoffrey Hill. Of these, the one which nearly "stuck" before old Geoffrey won was this, from the Gospel of Matthew:

> He said, "Go away; for the girl is not dead but sleeping."
> And they laughed at him.

Real hope is painful. To hope is to risk disappointment. If the hope is large enough, it even means to risk despair. And so, we find ways to avoid hope. For some, it is anger. For some, it is apathy. For some, it is laughter. After all, to laugh at a man who calls death sleep is the most rational thing in the world. Right?

During this period of writing, I often thought of another passage of scripture (which you will see when you come across the title poem later in this book). The promise in that passage is another absurdity, worthy of laughter. The idea is that somehow an eaten thing might come back, that it might be restored. Those words were written after years of an ancient famine, prompted by the devastation of vast clouds of locusts. Those years of the famine—with their work, their rhythm, their hope, their *life*—simply were gone. Like green shoots of barley, whose freshness and tender youth will never come again; *gone*. And yet, there was a promise. *I will restore to you the years that the locust hath eaten* . . .

In his story "The Garden of Forking Paths," Jorge Luis Borges places an excellent question in the mouth of a character: "In a riddle whose answer is chess, what is the only prohibited word?" The answer, of course, is simple. *Chess* is the only word that may not be used. While it may seem that the riddle of this book is about *grief* or *loss* or *lack*, or any number of things, it may be worth asking: *what is the word that may not be said in the riddle of this book?* (There is a word, a very common word, and it does not appear *even once* in these pages. That missing word is what this book is about.)

Enough then. Go read. I pray you glean something from the eaten field.

—PJP

The time is dark.
The time is wild.
So fill the lamp.
So guide the child.

The Springs

Atoms or systems into ruin hurl'd,
And now a bubble burst, and now a world.

—Alexander Pope

Skookumchuck

Broken the story, and broken the song,
Broken the river that bore us along,
Broken the cedars, and broken the shack,
Broken my wristwatch that cannot turn back.

Burnt is the hammock, and burnt is the moss,
Burnt is the Christ of the arsonist's cross,
Burnt are the seventeen hopes of my youth,
Burnt is my lying, and burnt is my truth.

Full is the junkyard, and full the crapmonger,
Full are the wheelchairs that wheelie no longer,
Full are the organs of stupid denial,
Full is each tear. And full every smile.

Famous our pleasure, and famous our fear,
Famous the ghosts that sing when we come near,
Famous that ocean that swallows our water,
And makes into sacrifice every slaughter.

Regarding Spring, Which Sharpens Grief by Means of Fresh, Unconquerable Joys

We find ourselves surrounded by the thing,
See it in flowers and our orchard trees.
The Lenten Roses bow like fasting souls,
The Bleeding Hearts lean breaking in the fog.
Pale plum buds that we peel with little knives
Show Christ's five wounds, each blossom like a brain.

Under our eaves, the robin's muddy nest
Spills raving chicks, each pricked by their half-quills.
The forest keeps close counsel, shrugs warm light,
The fawn's green rib blooms fungus in the rain.
Fresh moss chews shingles, shamed trees bow away,
And every little gift comes at a price.

Now when we walk, we walk as if we dream,
Understanding nothing, but knowing what it means.

Nehalem

I am a man from sullen counties
ranged along the low hills and the high,
variable of light, possessing many rains,
changeable of texture by each season.

Tides push up for miles in my rivers,
below red alders, undercut in roots
by brown streams full of rainbows and of lampreys;
sand flashes pyrite, kicked up by black snails.

Down dirt roads, houses tilt from their foundations
of cinder block, stacked wood, and auto jacks.
Bald tires have been laid upon their shingles
to still the ragged snapping of blue tarps,

and in them, always the loud, smeared tv,
damp rag rugs, warm-milk bowls of cereal,
the baby gates, the dogs' linoleum,
thrift-store guitars (impossible to tune),

and Pepsi children, chanting grand cartoons,
perpetually sniffing, crawling toward torn screens
to see whose car door slams out in the driveway,
below those clouds, possessing many rains,

and elk go by, all joyful in their bugling.
The hills lie breathing out their solemn dreams.
And I've become as variable as they—
just look, I am as changeable as they.

The Child's Teeth

> *Each to his own portion of Paradise,*
> *Stung by the innocent venoms of the earth.*
> —Geoffrey Hill

Now you who sense the dirges of the West,
Come here up the byways and the boulevards,
Borne by roads that knew the taste of hooves
And moccasins in better, lesser days,

Come to me here below the peregrines,
Leave your touchscreens, your cold garlic noodles,
To learn the membranes of our inner hides,
To mourn the fickle dead you cannot name.

Who have we been, that we should droop our eyes?
Out of the cumulus of grass, we rode lank ambition,
Until a dream of sugar and proud libraries
Loved itself to being, spoke its own name to God.

Young men quail before the blank particulates,
Wheezing melodies. Before we strike the brittle things,
Let there be fraternity and mute compassion;
What we can understand will never be for us.

And so, how has the gravel filled the bowl,
The sand sieved from the path, my jadeite cup,
As great against the sky the long light curls,
As small against the ground shrinks all our pride.

What May Not Be Accepted

Beautiful ground, beautiful hour,
Short the sun and long the shower.

Beautiful thought, beautiful word,
Quick the cat, and slow the bird.

Beautiful shade, beautiful light,
Short the day, and long the night.

Beautiful fall, beautiful spring,
How lately did those feathers sing.

The Mole

The mole that tubes the dirt
May be known by the plants
That bow above her work;
The soil trembles, heaves.

For on a secret road,
Her brute hands gouge long runes,
Mar quartzes and vast roots,
Hew temples in dark earth.

Now, underneath my life,
What burrows through the years?
My thoughts shake like tall grass—
Whose blunt claw digs my heart?

Here is a tiny dance; you cannot force it.

The snail you plucked up from the curling leaf
Now rests with fetal curve in your warm palm,
And waits for your heart's rhythm to drop slow
And stillness to well up within the hand

Like dew. Then out the lintel of the shell
Feel four exploring horns, long pinstalk eyes,
And patiently, rebuking every fault,
The arching of that foot begins to speak.

Of Bracken, and Other Natural Fractals, as an Image of the Unfurling Soul

The light, the low,
The stooped, the slow,
The way that ferns and crystals grow.

The harsh, the kind,
The marsh, the mind,
The kingdoms that the children find.

The trunk, the tree,
The hive, the bee,
The way the world is shaped like me.

The prick, the prayer,
The when, the where,
The way that there is something there.

The branch, the leaf,
The hand, the thief,
The way that we grow toward each grief.

The love, the grace,
The frond, the face,
The way I see you every place.

Up the Sun, Down the Moon

Should you rise to greet me,
hair braided, jingling with ornaments,
tell me you saw us dancing in a dream;
then that you slept again, praying to go back.

Should you see me at a port or in the station
through foggy glass, my red pack on my shoulders,
drop what you have brought, and run to kiss me;
every mile toward you has been cold and very long.

Should you catch your radiating eyes
debating windows, or a phone's blunted reflection,
don't cast down the temples of your brow;
in lost times, even glances are enough.

The Early Road

> *Charity itself is full of war.*
> —*Charles Péguy*

We broke out from the little hills at dawn,
The valley lain like plaid, with rippled seams
And horses at their fences like old men
Hemmed by slack memories of a taut world.

And whether it was real or in a thought
Is not the question. For the tar spooled forth,
And we drove out of time, with twenty men
In our two chests, a father and a son.

Here, always at the edge of something great,
We perch, but something welds us to the cliff,
And we don't move. At least, we do not leap,
But watch each other's lives pass quietly by—

So horses. So the cantering parade.
So barley in the stalk, all fresh and green,
So herons in black ditches, swearing *aye!*
And all the morning without any time.

And all the morning. Without any time.

Two Stanzas (for Emily)

In that April week
when soil sang
the blossom of the pear
and mason bees
investigated eaves,
all greens returned,
solemn and original.

Yes, and I saw you
barefoot in our garden,
everlasting in gray denim,
fussing with hellebores,
wordless, prayerful,
unaware of being
counted with the flowers.

Photosynthesis

When you have loved beyond your first horizons,
and have turned to your beloved and begun
to wonder who they have become,
under the verdigris of good, long years,

and when you learn to know the veritude
of glances, of every shared hour, of daily hands
that lay vast truths upon the hollows of your back,
and tremble under dark sheets in the night,

you will understand. Each green leaf
contains a billion mouths, which spin, which open,
hungry under sun. So with us, and so,
when such light falls on us for many years.

The Hope of Tears

We see the world with half-formed eyes and think
The world half-formed; that night falls when we blink.

Tears will wash the lens. The wise man's light
Is salt and hot. It makes each shadow bright.

The Noise of the Groat

There's no place like home, and home is no place
Quite like I dreamed back in those sunrise years
That countered every worry by blind grace
And did not know they held the kern of tears,
Whose root is love, which splits the barley's skull,
Whose early leaf is tender and so fresh,
But cannot guess the millstone's grinding pull,
Who has not learned yet what it means to thresh.
O Home, you field of bounty and of grief,
Make deep your furrows under God's flint plow,
And may you not fail the unshielded leaf
No one may guard, which yet is sprouting now.
And by rich gift, and by my hard-ground bone,
Grant that no seed which dies remains alone.

Who Has Been a Friend?

Who has been a friend?
—The wind.
It sighed when I have sighed.
It swept the fallen leaves,
And taught me how to breathe.
It died when I have died.

Who knew my desire?
—The fire.
It burned when I have burned.
It loved the incense wood.
Its cinders all glowed good.
It learned what I have learned.

Who taught me of my Father?
—The water.
It rained when I have rained.
We became wild streams.
We laughed about our dreams.
It gained what I have gained.

Who has had a wound?
—The ground.
It broke when I have bled.
And in its painful need
It brought forth much rich seed.
It fed whom I have fed.

The Summers

O you tender ones, step now and then
into the breath that takes no heed of you.

—Rainer Maria Rilke

Montana Seeds

For Eugene

Gone, I was the bristle in the brittle pines
Looped fractaling along the highway bends.
Mine were raw quills, of geese and porcupines;
Mine the rock brains; mine the trout-brown hands

That slapped wet prints upon the breaching stones;
A tremulous, confessing risk of joy;
The silver in the sockets of my bones;
The sun-bridge on the little wrestling bay.

I grew from roots of efficacious dreams.
I learned my name when others lost their own.
The precious glints all settled in my streams,
Most beloved when they were most unknown.

And in my stems, I trembled with the Christ,
Whose edges warbled me, by trunks, by resined cones
Shelved and seedy with a hundred dormant lives
Each, if undying, doomed to stay alone.

Because there is a life that does not live.
There is a death I know that does not die.
Hid down the streamy bends, with tipple and with give;
Bristling toward the pollens of our brittle pines.

Damascus Road

The light was violet, cinnabar, and green.
One cannot see what one has never seen.
I do not think you know quite what I mean.

The light was orange, somewhat-pink, and pink.
Christ dumped ball bearings on my roller rink.
I do not mean what you might think I think.

The light was purple, silvery, and teal.
I kicked the pricks so hard I could not feel.
I do not think that I was ever real.

The light was yellow, ebony, and blue.
The scales of some blind fishes rub off too.
I cannot think now, but I think of you.

Annus Mirabilis

And many bade him be quiet but he shouted all the more.
—Mark 10:48

It was the year of changes; of pyrite in the stream, and mica;
the year that it has been since we can remember.
And under the rusting swing, mason bees curved their blue jig
and played house in the cottonwood,
for it was the year of changes.
Forth from the woodshed, gaunt ants trooped spirals,
heralding rule to the barons of grasses.
The oriole mourned in her lilac's failed pagoda,
and poured new sorrows to the shrew,
for it was the only year she could remember.

Where now is your wisdom, my soul?
You are poor with losing; your right eye is plucked.
Where now is your boasting or your artifice?
They are fled like wind, past peeling vertebrae of houses.
And to whom shall you stumble, my soul?
For beyond the dead highway lies your lush and native country.
To whom will you complain, or rail old protestations?
You are in the problem; such may not be considered.
People look to you like walking trees;
the glass of your black tablet has been splintered.

But still, miracles tick toward us on the bee's bright dial;
ants perform their gamelan on neat bamboo.
The oriole's quenched sobs lift up fresh purple steeples,
and it is the only year we can remember.
There is no diminishing the bulk of hills,
except by little water for much time,
and all good things are hopeless, precisely when they are working.
Streams fill with grit and glitter; yes; mica, pyrite, gold.
The God of little things spits garnets in our mud.
For this is the year of changes. The year it has always been.

Where the Kildeer Runs

I have sometimes got so near to it that I could clearly see the pale red margin of its beautiful eye.
—*John J. Audubon*

I want to go back where the kildeer runs
and nurses her drooping wing,
to the orchards and fields and the summer shine
that shone over all your friends and mine,
back where the frogs and the brown snakes sing,
and the black-necked kildeer runs.

I want to go back where the kildeer runs
in the hollow, tawny fields,
to the sullen grapes and the summer barns
that opened their doors when we stretched our arms,
back where the wasps and the mantids wheel
and the tricky kildeer runs.

I want to go back where the kildeer runs
but I do not know the way,
so, I sit here and think in a looking-glass town
of all the kind hills that I wandered down,
where the child I am still hides and plays,
and the light hits slant in the long warm days,
and the paddocks sigh, and the slow sheep graze,
and the haunted kildeer runs.

Below the Glen

from notes written in the Gifford Pinchot National Forest

Let the silence get inside you. She needs
a place to nestle, with her tealing purr
you feel, but cannot hear, which umbers
louder as it sugars up your ribs.

And is that not the rumble of your need?
To drop the dulling fizz, the burdening
elocutable drone, which harries,
hammers with what you know might kill you

but to which you have resigned yourself.
No, let the silence get inside you. She is kind
and shaggy. She summons strange friends.
Her hands can teach the new and better languages.

American Isolate

Snake venom is used to cure snakebites!
    —*Tehching Hsieh*

First. Note the pattern of all growing things.
Each has an elegant unconsciousness
Calling that being to forget itself,
Preparing for the headlong gambling game
That blooms good shouts, sprouts clumped pubescent hair.
We laugh as voices crack; we jangle mirrors.

Next. Speculate upon the lacking thing
That binds our adolescent culture's roots.
What is the chain that cannot let us dance,
Even when rondels beckon our lean thighs?
Where does it hurt? We point to everywhere.
We stamp the toes of joy; *alone's* a verb.

Last. I have noted in some wild things
A confusing propensity to die.
Strong beetles levering off their carapace,
Crows that slam windows repeatedly.
The worm that leaves damp soil for dry sand.
They're trying everything. Like you, like me.

Wringing the Changes

I have known the breathless feeling of a sponge that has been wrung
Thoroughly and roughly above my life's chipped sink,
Squeezed to the point of tearing by the chapped hands of God
Until my shape was nothing. Until I could not think.

I have known the way one squishes at the crushing of one's foam,
Have felt the curious balling of a thing without a spine.
But all of it led to a hope I do not hold alone:
That when my water's all pressed out, I might soak in his wine.

Wild Currants, *or*
How Sorrow is the School of Wisdom

Red currants, in their royal summer way
Are playacting at rubies in the shrubs.
And toward them, all the purple finches play,
Jousting at sticks and trumping up the grubs
Who populate the darkened underthings.
I knew that I was undone when I sat
In silence and I liked it, like a king
Who feels his crown is just a workman's hat
And all his sovereign duty's dull and long.
Come fair, come foul—come and ply your arts.
Pluck berries, worms, and stuff them in that song.
There will be cold nights soon. They'll shrive our hearts,
Until the soul down low wakes up to keep
Its counsel with strong wisdom now asleep.

On Wasted Time

In the temple of lost hours
there are paintings on the cool walls

of what might have been made
from days now long made permanent, and

brushing them, you understand. You see
your life, a unique, fragile trapezoid

you tried to fold symmetrically; a bag of water
which you pierced all night with little pins; you

look until the door slams to the middle balustrades
and you remember why you came here first, and when.

Zoetrope of Paul

The tanagers. The columbine.
The Rorschach sediments of wine.

The grit of my unshaven cheek.
The soil of the blessed meek.

The shocks of gray that root my hairs.
The words that I mistook for prayers.

The nip upon the dog's pink lip.
The perfect curve of my wife's hip.

The tan balloon of a dead deer.
The carboy foaming with new beer.

The trampled books our children read.
The lettuce bolting back to seed.

The car. The corn. The baby born.
Last night. The everlasting morn.

Chariot of Elijah

Time released me from him as I could not have . . .
    —Geoffrey Hill

Some weaknesses are prompts for charity.
What if the flame from which those wheels were hewn
Was not, all told, an honor for that man
Who'd crumbled before angels in the broom

And eaten ravens' generosity?
The cumuli retreat, the blue veil parts
With thunder of electric axles rolled.
Our throats are pushing down against our hearts.

Was it a gift to be spared death's indignity?
Or did God simply in compassion scry
That sometimes even prophets lack the strength
To fail, to end, to say that one goodbye?

Notes For a Poem (To a Dead Friend)

Have I been faithless to your memory,
Who died before our beards had come full in?
We who'd buzzed our hair short in the yard,
And punched each other's arms until they bruised?
Our falling out was from a dozen things.
You mocked me secretly to the wrong friend,
I thought myself the better of the pair,
And on. So, years went by until the call
In which somebody told me you were sick,
And wished for visitors. I never went.
We buried you behind the white board church.
Your mother too, a few years afterward.
There was a rusting fence. A walnut tree.
There was you underground, and there was me.

On Wauna Lake

Three geese confer in loud debate
about the sun. From Table Mountain
the old, intelligible gods once made a bridge
to span the black Columbia for two lovers.

There are waves. Pink lilies root in shallows.
The invisible sturgeon, connoisseur of silt,
feeds deliciously. In little bays,
stones roll to bathe in the green waves.

Wind; water; time; the earth breathes
up and down; the lightning brings the fire.
The bridge of the gods fell; the lovers are dead,
but we are still talking about them.

Of a Hermit Thrush

Her whistle is climbing its spiral stair
and loath are my evenings, loath of bone,
and fir trees are steeples in the air,
and every confession is told alone.

The little lung beats the feathered snare,
and fair is my sunset, fair of light,
and here bends the proverb, the tricky prayer,
and I sit and I know the quieting night.

The Night Garden

> *"... in strange Christian hope, go down*
> *into the darkness of resurrection ..."*
>
> —*Geoffrey Hill*

Wonderful things are happening here.
The snake bellies up to the still-warm stone.
One star settles into the crook of the tree.
But everything dreaming must dream alone.

I smoke tobacco under a moon
Whose face gawps down with a carnival stare
To watch the divisions of moth and bat.
The pear tree brushes her silver hair,

And I think of each of my trying days.
I burn my thumb with a broken match
And the cat in the hedge has a knowing look
As I curse the soft thoughts people stuff in books,
Because the night garden brings everything near
And wonderful things are happening here.

Under the Perseids

I sit and watch the evening in the West
As day slacks off the dial of the sun
And fades in stars; Venus, first and best,
Followed by Mars, the only honest one,

And then the show. The heavens twitch and fall
By crumbs and sparks, each burning like a breath
With no hope of return. They teach us all
That every light we see is something's death.

The Dream

I woke, and all the kingless world was bleak.
I slept, and earth was governed by the meek.

I woke, and there was roaring from the south.
I slept, and children stopped the lion's mouth.

I woke, and saw the locust eat the wheat.
I slept, and wept before the mercy seat.

I know I sojourn in the land of seem.
But which is real, my God? And which the dream?

Crosses

The Carpenter's was made of wood.
The Mother's was her son.
So it is with everyone.
With everyone.

What we hold dear is laid on us.
Then we are laid on it.
And down us run the blood and spit.
The blood and spit.

The lover's cross is made of love.
Someone's is made of me.
God's cross is made of all we see.
Of all we see.

The Falls

no, nothing is empty, but it's something like empty

—Jon Fosse

Phantom Limb

The wound is in the amputated thing,
The ghost of happening,
The ghost of pain.

Now what is gone no longer is your own,
But you can keep the feeling,
The stump of bone.

Who dares to say that you can't touch the sun?
You span all distance now,
Reach far past anyone.

The Alembic

All that you see will fall back into earth,
Surrender form, drain slow through secret halls,
Trickle down stone of caverns underground,
Where crystals seep like milk in lightless caves;

All that you see will filter and distill
Until the single drop of it presumes
To shiver and to fall in the clear dreams
Which pool beneath our feet, which all souls drink.

There waits the perfect spirit of the world,
Whose alembic is loss, whose still is time,
And whose keen drip we even now can hear:
Below, below, below. Be low. Be. Low.

The Locust Years

I will restore to you the years that the locust hath eaten.
—*Joel 2:25*

My son, there is no fairness in the years,
No paid deserving. Nothing but the gift
Gone forth, gone sideways. Nothing but the pain
Of wandering, trying all within the locust years,

And evermore the crisping, as those leaves
Are lost by decades, like the salmon-feathered months
Whose calendars buzz promises, filling, emptying,
Whistling in the wind like eaten leaves.

But there will come an autumn day when highway lines
Point home, return you to the gravel drive
Cut in the hedge, the wet road filling, emptying,
Pulling you to me with highway lines,

And I will trot to greet you, all the swarming years
Behind us, run like you would when I pulled in view
When we were younger, you a toddy boy, I less grizened wild
From all the wrack and weeping of the locust years.

Then we will pitch gold pippins in the press,
Crank them to cider. Strain skully sweetness free
Of flesh and skin, the arsenic of seeds;
Push-pulling, each of us, the handle of the press,

And you will not suspect it when I rough your hair,
But I will then be thinking of the day
When by my last bed you will kneel, and cry
And laugh and kiss me; smooth my grizened hair.

Because there is no fairness in the years,
No paid deserving. But still sweetness fills the pot
As press lets forth our froth, as we both laugh and crank,
And crush the gift to toast our locust years.

For V. the Bag Lady, Great in the Kingdom of Heaven

You'd have to smell the potluck food she brought.
It likely turned. The lukewarm food bank cheese,
Or last month's beef gleaned from behind the store
Would knock you back. Nobody said a word.
She moved in floral mumus like a queen.
She had no teeth. She'd squeak in from the rain
To shed her mildewed layers by her pew,
And make hot chocolate in cheap styrofoam.
Years later, I was hard up out at school.
Two jobs, bill due, and eight bucks in the bank.
Somehow, she heard. Her father had just died.
Left her ten grand. And she gave half to me.
I still can see her lift her hands to sing.
In them, I watched her lifting everything.

Because I Thought That Hope Was Not for Me

Because I thought that hope was not for me,
I missed it in the gutters of the street,
And in the dyings of the compost heap.

For hope nests drowsy in dark soil and peeks
Rat-like from out brown broken glass and squeaks
Its echoes in the hollows of the meek.

So now I sob for it, and sometimes shriek,
And I shall laugh at secrets like a freak,
And I shall learn to bless my eyes and see,
And I shall let hope nest and nuzzle me.

The Visitation

The angel who had come to bind my wounds
Seemed stoic and depressed. His tight-cropped hair,
Cowlicked as if frequently helmeted,
Was completely passé; in luster dull,
In color like the damp sand of low tide.
The oil and the linen in his hands
Were beautiful, but held no miracles,
Beyond the wonder of their presence there.
I had limped toward the alleyway of sleep
With tears and gut roll, agonies of psalms,
As demons peeped from ceilings and through walls
With gargy grins, who dinked with vertebrae,
Until he came, in answer to no prayer,
Just said, "You are attended," and stood there.

Blue Bandana

I thought I knew what prayer was
in the young, good days that smelled of mint and dill,
in the crushing of the sesame within the mill,
I thought I knew what prayer was.

Then there was a shaking in the underground
and through the crack that rived the bedrock stone
shone the pink glow, luminous, alone,
freed by the shaking in the underground,

and I became persuaded to a joy
whose knowledge was the knowledge of deep dark
turned sideways by the presence of one spark,
and I became persuaded to a joy.

The Garden of Abu Ghosh

*But their eyes were holden
that they should not know him.*

—*The Gospel of Luke*

I stood once, at the gateway of your heart,
Knowing the father-word to open locks,
Ready for a lifetime of the joy
Of being known; of knowing you, my boy.

But in the earth and water moved the rust
To strip your hinges; leave the lockbolt dry
And I stood waiting, wordless and afraid
As so much life was quietly unmade.

And then the fury of the blank-eyed storm,
Which whipped our faces till the skin was rough
And tears were rare, so deep had gone the grief
And we watched every day move like a thief.

In the dark garden now, I see you walk,
And sometimes that can be enough for me.
I still stand at the gateway of your heart.
I will die standing; I cannot depart.

I Must Become as Beautiful as Kelp

I must become as beautiful as kelp
Drawn leggy down a brown, foamed beach
After the king tide. Bulbed and full of thoughts,
I have desired to become like kelp.

For there are lives that root themselves in seas,
Yearn daily upward, toward cathedral light
That nourishes slow leaves that no winds blow,
Waving in the sieve of the numb seas.

I have desired my tough effervescent stalk
To grow and lengthen, hold me to my place
While lighter things pool up in me and reach
For the lean sun, where spirit trawlers stalk.

I shall become as elegant as kelp,
Dancing in these currents of our seas,
Held down, pulled up, here to be each to each,
Until I rise, and I am given to the beach.

By This You'll Know It's Love

You'll nurse the garden where the locust played
And see each might-have-been. You'll rack your days
For minutes absent of those tough-break ways.
You'll thank the helpless air for having stayed
When earth's unquestioned pillars fell away.
You'll know your losses in the bleak arcade
Where all the games were promises you made.
All this. And still you'll come back every day.

Sawgrass Song

Ocean Park, Washington

Where there is water
and the plump gulls gliding,
where the brine's tang
slips the curlew from her marsh,
I have become sharp
through the sky's free dullness;
I learn the gamboled striding
of the violent, jolly Earth.

Where there is water
and the torn crabs drying,
drawn and pinkly quartered
for the beige, opulent waste,
I have become keen
as pipers, as coyotes;
I learn my weight by turning
toward my track back on the sand.

Where there is water
and the barked logs rolling,
where the sawgrass
holds the dune down by its root,
I have become still
in my memory of losing;
I learn the gifted grieving
of the one left on the shore.

A Small Defiance

The manufacturers of empty thoughts
Whose pillow is the coin, whose bed the cloud,
Have massed themselves, arrayed in endless clots,
Have mustered up the tedious and loud,

But I defy them, in their vast display,
To touch me, in my body or my head.

Gathering up my will, to them I say
That I shall live, though their whole world fall dead.

In the Fall

When I was sixteen, and my six-string heart
Had learned to fret full chords below my neck,
I used to wander. Down the railroad grade
To the dead mill, abandoned to the trees,
Whose vengeance cast the cement temples down.
A maze of spray paint and of startled quail,
Of mattresses dragged into roofless rooms,
Of salmon casting milt down in the creek,
And alders, slowly dropping their damp cones,
A place of soggy titty mags, malt cans,
And cigarillos, half-smoked, stamped upon
With the quick disappointments of the young,
Whose eagerness to sin is innocence.
I walked through, where the roots heaved cracking slabs,
And crows pulled laces free from rotten boots,
And all around me spoke the secret thing;

"Beware, sweet fools—you change the world with you."

The Oracle

She always speaks too little or too late.
Never has lied, but always puts the truth
So on the lean that touch it, and it tips.
She wears a blindfold as she paints her lips.

You go to her when desperate and alone.
Up from her navel comes the platinum word
That cleaves you like a plum clean to the middle.
You see your pit reflected in her riddle.

Of course you wish to read these wracking limbs,
Find sense among the entrails of your life.
But you will be bad burned by each bright spark.
Some lights are falser than an honest dark.

The demon speaks. You offer nuts and dimes.
The smoke goes up. You leave. The statue grins.
And you will come again. You will forget.
Because you do not trust the silence yet.

On Crucifixion as Holding One Open from the Instinctive Fetal Position of the Wounded

A motion so familiar, childlike.
The beetle does it. So the soldier boy,
Balling to protect his gutshot core
Until there is no hoping anymore.

Because we all are infants when we hurt,
Returning to first pain, first cold, first cry,
And waiting to be held by someone strong
And mewling that we might not wait too long.

And so observe those three exacting pins
That fix one, like a moth stretched on a board,
The elbows cracked into a wide embrace,
The legs nailed straight to mock the lolling face.

The heart itself less intimate and raw
Than that pierced paunch, where belly drools its gobs,
And how one wants to curl and staunch the flow,
At least say *please stop* as the dark floods go,

But even that last comfort is denied.
Held open to the sky, and naked splayed
Whose work of pain grows fruitful, like a tree.
Our skewered Lord thus showed the world to me.

That Which Cannot Rest Content

Suppose there was a king who loved a humble maiden.
         —*Søren Kierkegaard*, Philosophical Fragments

And in the king's kind chest, suppose an anxious thought,
Which counsel or rebuke could not dispel; suppose
The nibbled notion that his favor, once conferred,
Would sour like stale wine on last night's table,
That sudden transport up the social mountain
(The bride bathed quick in milk, dried hurriedly with sables)
Might taint the downy thing that had turned magnet pole,
Pulling heart's red needle; suppose the torment of the helpless throne,
Loosing headsmen in gaunt, teary rage, dividing vertebrae
Of any fool suggesting tilted unions do not herald joy;
Suppose this all stood fable for your own well-threshed sorrows:
Now bowing under barley-weight of over-fruitful life,
Now rousing the nude grief that sleeps, delicate, in love.

Lachrymae Mundi

He ran shallow, like the creeks.
He knew the company of freaks.

He ran lazy, like the river.
He knew men who killed their liver.

He ran mighty, like the sea.
He knew nobody was free.

He ran down the glass, like rain.
He knew plum pits and all pain.

He ran down God's crying cheek.
He knew the spring. He fed the creek.

Cherry On, Lost John

The world is not so sideways in its luck as people say;
there still are futures of a healthful gain;
rain still rains.

Lichens droop from spruces, wizard-gray,
there are yet handsome gambles in the living game;
rain still rains.

Below the dust crust, we strike water in the hushing cave;
crystals lengthen, treasuring the downward way;
rain still rains.

The world is not so startled in its lack as people say;
we find lively flowers in the long decay;
rain still rain still rains.

Haunting

Would be enough to gust this waking wood,
rippled with the dapple of the deer,
shade among shades, fluidlike and good,
forgetting the existences of fear,
glass, and money. Changing with the light,
passing past the burling of the trees
like smoke in summer, elemental, slight,
constrained by nothing but the silken breeze
and memory. Enough to know I'm bound
as ever to the champings of this place,
heady with the loaming of the ground,
heavy with the misting of the grace.
I'm limboed, lost and happy under oaken galls.
Found here a haven, should my prayers hit false.

Hunting

A white doe in the green grass of a glade
Appeared to me with two horns made of gold.
—*Petrarch*

All joy, being considered in its truth,
Has in it both the terrible and good.
You will not know the beauty of the deer
Until you've laid her low within the wood.

All joy, being rejected for its pain,
Has in it both the brutal and the kind.
You will not know the virtuous or wise
Until you purge perfection from your mind.

Grinding the Peppercorns

Bearing witness to the essential virtues,
I have come to the plateau of my life
confounded by my contours
and quartzite dissipations,

yet optimistic. I've glimpsed
the hump of Faith, which rolled the algal wave,
sought Hope's imperfect pelt upon the game trail,
had Love stop me with a sharpened bone

dipped in mashed ink of gall-wasps,
clucking: *someone must mark you,
little man. Let it be me*, and I saw,
and I saw, and I breathed.

Growing Late

The keeping of appearances,
The sense of passing time,
The way the hours rhyme,
The weakening of differences.

The solstices each have their twin,
And so each equinox.
Go chase for us the fox,
Then kill the light as we begin.

Our compass will point south one day,
The magnets will swap poles,
As actors end their roles,
Reverse their face and slip away.

Here, I am left holding your hand
Against the patient wind.
Was it this man who sinned?
But how? I cannot understand.

The Winters

La souffrance passe, mais le fait d'avoir souffert ne passe jamais.
Suffering passes, but having suffered never passes.

—Léon Bloy

The Winter Bank

The starved sun on the wet black rock,
The white wind on the river.
The eagle tears the salmon's jaw
And I lean with the weather.

The broken glass is green and brown.
The raccoons pile shells.
And I learn wonders no one knows;
At least which no one tells.

The Watch

You who sit in buildings
in the lost hours, sit up

rocking a little, soothing
your brain's pressed spring;

you who witness worries
ballooning in proportion

then crack full,
snapping like black sails;

you who wait like me
to notice useless dawn

or to welcome
second sleep's sleek purring;

you are good company,
though you are far and quiet,

though we'll never know
we woke beside each other.

Staying

That clock whose long hand is the setting sun,
Whose short hand is the moon, whose face the sky,
Whose gears are wound each year by God's bright key,
Which chimes each spring with birds sprung from the tree,
That clock whose pendulum inscribes the sea,
Has stopped for you, dear one. But not for me.

Every Upping is a Down

The dark of winter dawn,
The aptitude of night,
And every setting moon has mirrored
The morning in its light.

Now day comes like a riddle,
A nickel's worth of grace,
And I can feel the rising sun
Reflected in my face.

A Song for Late in Time

Nothing true, nothing simple,
Nothing wondrous, nothing good,
Nothing that is left to wander,
Nothing to be understood.

Nothing kind, nothing brutal,
Nothing like the grinding mill,
Nothing sullen, nothing gracious,
Nothing left for us to kill.

Nothing silent, nothing angry,
Nothing like the bottled flies,
Nothing thorny, bald, or wrinkled,
Nothing like the upcast eyes.

Nothing shouting, nothing falling,
Nothing in the apple tree,
Nothing lives behind the woodwork,
Nothing presses up on me.

Nothing wise, nothing stupid,
Nothing looks back in the mirror.
Nothing like a silent river.
Nothing flows away from here.

Science of Relations

> *Those first-born affinities that fit*
> *Our new existence to existing things....*
> —*William Wordsworth, "Prelude"*

I think these gentle days are the most cruel:
my little sections of the pleasant hours
which separate like ripened tangerines,
or pass like barges below evening cliffs,
pleading light to the Columbia;

little sections, yes, of pleasant hours
which refract and slip like neon jewels
before the moon's various mirrors,
as if God was a child, shaking earth's kaleidoscope,
having first removed you from the tube.

The worst is how I rarely cry
about you anymore, an acceptance
that says *permanent betrayal*.
Mathematic moments pass, quite like before
when you could still be called or visited,

my little sections (yes!) of pleasant hours
that I should not stand and rejoice in,
though you'd whack my arm and say to *get on living*,
tell a worn joke you'd said so much before
that it comforted with tedium, like life.

The selfsame twilight can appear both dark and light.
Depends if you compare the night or day
to its halfway appearing.
The last glimpse we can discern white threads from black
is the moment to prepare to end the fast.

Everything must rest on something else,
whole planets can be moved by just one ant,
every color pulls the spectrum round.
We only see the redness of the red
because we see the greenness of the green.

I expect I'll still be here next year
watching titmice flicker the gray banks,
watching white oaks earn costly yards
against black firs, lavishing nuts
to swamp the mousehands of the fallen cones.

I will be here, seeing faces in the moon,
accepting that all beauties are betrayals
in allegiance to a larger thing than life.
I sometimes glimpse it as the colors shrink
to describe new angles, serving vast geometries.

This is that; this is not that,
That is that; that is not this,
This is this, and all the sundry
logics tell the story just as well.
The science of relations is a spell.

Who is *we*? *We* are who,
who we are is we, who
fling our colors patiently toward mirrors.
The more I lose, the more I learn the game.
The science of relations is a name.

Advice

Forsake all Beauty if you can,
and from her truth break free,
for in an age of ugly things
the good brings misery.

But if her spear is in your spleen
and you can't shake her off,
then give your life for love of her
and count that good enough.

Gap of the Hedge

The laurels by the road have been
ripped ragged by December,

the smallest now uprooted
by the fury of the wind

and angry as the socket
where a tooth has been torn loose,

the little tipply juncos
are flying through the wound

and the wind is patient, pulling
at two laurels on the gapsides

which wobble in the wet earth
heavy with their leaves,

and I will stand here thinking
for a moment of my morning

of how much we each are weakened
when any neighbor falls.

Snowed In

The snow has swelled to lick the windowsill
With its dead tongue. The luxury of chill
Has favored every creaking of the eaves.
The laurel hedge regrets its emerald leaves.

All things are either torpid or they shake.
The wind carves drifts like some ghost's birthday cake.
And everything stands naked, bony, true.
Somehow, it's all not half as cold as you.

Surely, a Well Feels like a Wound to the Earth?

Draw up, child of this soil,
water from the dark below you.
Pull down light from such places
as you can, keen and in quantity.

The silence trembles in its finite egg.
What shall you do with it, and when?
Wait a little. Not everyone who will learn
to love you has yet been born.

The Cameo

Friend, tell me of these changes of the light.
Great vigors and low lassitudes of grief
Were carved under bleak agencies of night
Into your cheek, in high and sharp relief—
And tell me of your loss. Which fatal turn
Embossed you with those raven's feet of grace?
And what mouth smiles through yours? And help me learn
Whose silhouette is mimicked in your face?
Because resemblance is a truthful lie
And every shadow shows out wild pasts;
A mother's nose, that cavern of an eye,
The hair that fades, the skull's high dome that lasts,
And all of it, within the carbon glory,
Is whispering an ancient, holy story.

Let Us Keep the Feast

Begin to sing the song when you
Have lost the rhythm of your life.
The tepid guards of taste and mind
Have nothing to keep you in time.

You can become your fabled end,
With bones of gold, with eyes of water,
Moving through the ruined places
To shelter in eternal graces.

The tepid guards? How can so few
Lever great shoulders out of joint?
Their blindness forces you to see
Their infinite emergency.

Allow your movement to ascend
To mimicry. The flowering pear,
The jays that twitch the cursing air,
The denizens of everywhere

Are teaching you how to survive
The toxic and conditional.
You cannot know your ending yet.
You can remember to forget.

St. Erzsébet Daydreams of a Lost Swallow

Balassi Stanzas

The love that set my bed
beneath the leper fed
many. (Mouths like dark roses.)
The poor you always have,
he said. It's true. In drab
turns they breed. The rich closes
eye to their pecked wracks.
Perhaps grudges limp sacks
of poppy seeds. God knows his

own though. Good potters throw
punches in flopped clay, do
what's best (what's best looks too rough),
allowing no cover,
leaning, panting over
each slouched lump, wheeled fast, wheeled tough
until slid in red kiln.
Dear Christ, rip my thick film!
Crack me wide to sing: *enough*.

For enough you must be.
It is no robbery
to move spare bread around.
The love that set my bed
beneath the leper fed
many. (Mouths like soft ground.)
Horsemen and their horn bows
fall silent in high snows.
But the swallow's lost song sounds.

I Have Visited the Country on the Other Side of Grief

I have visited the country on the other side of grief,
played in its copper fountains, memorized the streets
that cut the silent forest to the luminescent sea;
I have visited the country on the other side of grief.

I found your face reflected in the puckers of the moon
that rose to frost the mountains; christened clouds by sheets,
and shut the violent chorus up with adolescent key,
I found your face reflected in the puckers of the moon.

I lost myself forever in the beauty of that sea
whose renegades and captains have banded in their fleets,
healthiest when sorest pressed to give a name to me.
I have visited the country on the other side of grief.

Too Quick the Thaw

And now we see the hidden rage of ice
Flood fields, flush up the molewife from her den,
That horseish nature as the water bucks,
Spooked and trampling toward the river bend,

Every gutter moaning on our house,
Every gully sending tribute down,
Galloping to where the water froths
And bobbing up whole birches in the brown,

And now we watch the snow fort on the lawn
Shrinking in a sudden moat of green;
The snowman dribbles, staring at my face,
Mouths: *all too fast you will be joining me.*

Exchange Rate

A child would take a hundred hours
and swap them for a hundred dollars.

But how much would a rich man spend
for that time as a child again?

Severing Road

I.

Here trips a scene that plays in every age:
The tilting mother, heavy in those clogs,
Her man's strong lean. Half-guilty, how could he
For even one slogged mile swap their lots?
Wishes he could. So grateful he cannot.

II.

I know this pair. I've seen them on my street,
And on the lightrail in the bluish glow,
Or in last pews, and (thrice) in my own mirror.
Their details change, like paint smeared in the rain,
But as they go, their shape remains the same.

III.

Between their heads, always that curving love
That welcomes the strange one, knows oily sheens
Of mud. Her ankles carrying for two,
The man's cupped elbow steadying three (all),
Four eyes that seek a door in every wall.

IV.

I'd like to think that I would pull them in,
Cook noodles, shake some chicken in the wok,
But probably not. I'd be responsible.
Our loneliest all cling to one another.
Someone outside is yelling: *"Look, your mother!"*

V.

So with gaunt grace, the grand nativity
Keeps slouching past. The window shades uncoil,
Pharmacies post guards, men chain the dogs.
Our judgment kicks, so patient and so curled.
Our slow salvation trundles through the world.

Some lines written after realizing that time may be simply a vast loom, and our lives its colored threads.

Come thin, come thick, the world will be the world.
What lives will live. The dying thing will die.
From out the hips of roses bloom their pregnancies of thorns,
And all will tell; the world will be the world.

Come flak, come fling, the truth will be the truth.
Who knows will know. The fools will multiply.
From out the knees of puppets jerk the elemental strings,
And all will laugh; the truth will be the truth.

Come rough, come red, the love will be the love.
What yearns will yearn. The giving thing will give.
From out the dreams of pilgrims comes the road that leads them home.
And we will find; the love will be the love.

To One Who Would Mourn Me

Only be sad for little things, my love;
The good cup cracked, the picnic quenched by rain,
And only weep for what your will might change.

This is not strange.

And let the large griefs lighten you, my love;
You have a friend who has gone on before.
You must not look with longing toward the door.

There will be more.

Talus

And all our time is coming down to this,
Where moss extends its hidden root to find
In freeze, in thaw, the widening of cracks;
Some purchase for the holding of a life,

As in the jagged fields the pikas cheep
Among the mazes of the fallen stone
Ancient with our wedged geometry,
And heavy as our memories of home.

No one says what breaks us in the end,
But break we will, in sharpened basalt angles
And all our time is coming down to this—
As our hearts shed their rock, we comfort angels.

The Sower

I will reject my hope of good result,
And kindle corn into the sullen sod,
Push treasure to the narthex of the worm,
Measure out dark furrows in the yard

As I have done for years before this one,
With patient loss of time and clean belief,
Watching the sprouted seeds each droop and fail,
Be shredded, pucked-on, fiddled down by feet.

For hope and folly's boundary lines are thin.
Idiots and believers share a bed
Too short for stretching on; and how
I still can do this, I don't know, but I—

But do I *do*, and with a love of it,
Packing earth under my broken nails,
And looking for that dear face in the dirt
To send up shoots; to praise the eaten years.

Acknowledgments

This book would never have been made without the love and careful work of many people besides myself.

They include, but are not limited to: my wife Emily, my literary agent Whitney Gossett, the entire staff of Wiseblood Books (especially Joshua Hren and Mary Finnegan), the faculty and students of the Master of Fine Arts Program at the University of St. Thomas in Houston, Texas, with special thanks to James Matthew Wilson, Ryan Wilson, Seth Wieck, Timothy Kleiser, Carla Galdo, Jeff Young, Mary Grace Mangano (who gave the manuscript an especially generous early read), Dorian Speed, Lesley Clinton, Maya (Clubine) Venters, and all the beloved students of that first cohort; The Garden Party (Leslie Williams and Abigail Carroll), who were the first readers of many of the poems here; the various editors who selected or encouraged individual poems, including A. M. Juster, Leon Wieseltier, Celeste Marcus, Conor Sweetman, Mary Ann Miller, Whitney Rio-Ross, and others; and my many literary friends and acquaintances whose attention in various ways, large and small, encouraged me during this process. They include Christian Wiman, A. E. Stallings, J. C. Scharl, Marly Youmans, Sally Thomas, Justin Whitmel Earley, K. J. Ramsey, Malcolm Guite, and *so* many others whose help or presence, near or far, gave something to me.

I would also like to "see" each of my children: Elaia, Emmaus, and Marko, whose presence has been the greatest gift to me that I can imagine, and who are loved by me beyond words.

A doubly special word of thanks is due to Michael Cook. I have worked with many talented individuals, but never with one whose very *soul* seemed to flow so freely, purely, and generously through paint and pencil. I am humbled to have his rich art accompany my words.

And thanks, eternally, to the Creator. "Like a moth you eat away all that is dear to us" (Psalm 39:12). Even that eating is perfectly and wholly *love*. All praise to you, now and to ages of ages.

PJP

First Publication Credits

"Skookumchuck" first appeared in *Christianity and Literature*, a quarterly journal of the Conference on Christianity and Literature, published by Johns Hopkins University Press.

"Montana Seeds," "Cherry On, Lost John," and "Wringing the Changes" first appeared in the Poet's Corner of *The North American Anglican*.

"Annus Mirabilis" and "Regarding Spring, Which Sharpens Grief by Means of Fresh, Unconquerable Joys" first appeared in *Plough*.

"Below the Glen" first appeared in *Fathom*.

"American Isolate" first appeared in *U.S. Catholic*.

"The Locust Years" first appeared in *Presence*.

"Snowed In" first appeared in *The New Verse Review*.

"That Which Cannot Rest Content" won second place in a contest at *Dappled Things*, first appeared there, and was anthologized in *Homage to Søren Kierkegaard*, edited by Dana Gioia and Mary Grace Mangano, and published by Wiseblood Books.

Several poems here will, in theory, have been published by *Liberties* by the time of this collection's publication. They are "The Oracle," "Of a Hermit Thrush," "Notes for a Poem (To a Dead Friend)," and "Hunting."

Various other poems appeared as early drafts for the first time in *The Rose Fire*, Paul's newsletter.

Minor line edits have been made to the above poems for their appearance in this collection, compared to their first publication.

About the Author

Paul J. Pastor was born in Portland, Oregon on New Year's Day, under Halley's Comet. He is a widely-published writer and poet, and serves as an Executive Editor for Nelson Books, an imprint of HarperCollins. He lives in Oregon.

About the Artist

Michael Cook's paintings and drawings are in the Neo-romantic tradition in British art, where the landscape suggests the inner world of the artist. He is the owner of The Manger Gallery, a converted 19th century stable, which celebrates contemporary narrative painters and works of the romantic and religious imagination. He lives in Derbyshire, England.

Connect with Paul

Should you wish, you may write to Paul at

> Paul J. Pastor
> P.O. Box 36,
> Bridal Veil, OR 97010

You can also connect with Paul online at

> www.pauljpastor.com
> pauljpastor.substack.com
> x.com/pauljpastor

Connect with Michael

You can connect with Michael online at

> www.hallowed-art.co.uk
> instagram.com/michaelcookartist

About Wiseblood Books

If you loved this book, we know you will enjoy other titles from the Wiseblood Books catalog. There, you will find fiction, poetry, and monographs from a number of America's most accomplished literary writers including Dana Gioia, Marly Youmans, Sally Thomas, Alfred Nicol, Rhina P. Espaillat, James Matthew Wilson, Katy Carl, and many more. In supporting this hardworking independent press, and the talented authors who publish through it, you will be participating in the good work of promoting new literature and our mission to foster works of fiction, poetry, and philosophy that wrestle us from the ruse of distraction; find redemption in uncanny places and people; articulate faith and doubt in their incarnate complexity; dare an unflinching gaze at human beings as "political animals"; and render well this world's sufferings without forfeiting hope—all of this with wide eyes.

Review our catalog and purchase directly at wisebloodbooks.com, or request a copy of any of our books from your favorite bookseller.

You can also help other readers find *this* book by giving a copy to a friend, suggesting it for a reading group, requesting the title for your local library, sharing your response via social media, or by writing and publishing a review.

We are grateful for your support in building a rich culture of contemporary literature.